ASIA-PACIFIC

2008-9 NMI MISSION EDUCATION RESOURCES

✣ ✣ ✣

BOOKS

AFRICA
Where the Decades Still Whisper
by Robert Perry

ASIA-PACIFIC
From the Rising of the Sun
by Brent Cobb

THE CARIBBEAN
A Legacy of Love
by Keith Schwanz

EURASIA
Bountiful Blessing
by R. Franklin Cook, Gustavo Crocker, Jerald D. Johnson, and T. W. Schofield

MEXICO AND CENTRAL AMERICA
A Tapestry of Triumph
by Tim Crutcher

SOUTH AMERICA
A Harvest of Holiness
Compiled by Christian Sarmiento

✣ ✣ ✣

ADULT MISSION EDUCATION RESOURCE BOOK

100 YEARS OF MISSIONS
Editors: Aimee Curtis and Rosanne Bolerjack

ASIA-PACIFIC
from the rising of the sun

brent cobb

Nazarene Publishing House
Kansas City, Missouri

Copyright 2008
Nazarene Publishing House

ISBN 978-0-8341-2344-1

Printed in the United States of America

Editor: Aimee Curtis
Cover Design: Adam Jackman
Interior Design: Sharon Page

Unless otherwise indicated, all Scripture quotations are taken from the *Holy Bible, New International Version®* (NIV®). Copyright © 1973, 1978, 1984 by International Bible Society. Used by permission of Zondervan Publishing House. All rights reserved.

From the *Holy Bible, New Living Translation* (NLT), copyright © 1996. Used by permission of Tyndale House Publishers, Inc., Wheaton, IL 60189. All rights reserved.

Scripture quotations that are marked RSV are from the *Revised Standard Version* (RSV) of the Bible, copyright 1946, 1952, 1971 by the Division of Christian Education of the National Council of Churches of Christ in the USA. Used by permission.

Scripture quotations that are marked KJV are taken from the *King James Version*.

10 9 8 7 6 5 4 3 2 1

Dedication

To Dr. Donald and Adeline Owens, mentors, first American Nazarene missionaries to Korea, founders of Korea Nazarene University, first Asia-Pacific regional director couple, founders of Asia-Pacific Nazarene Theological Seminary, and the first general superintendent couple under whom I served as Asia-Pacific regional director

Contents

Foreword	9
Introduction	11
1. The Sun of Righteousness Shining in Japan	15
2. Rays of Hope for Chinese People	23
3. A Light for the Nations Shining from Korea	32
4. Beautiful Beams Radiating from the Philippines	38
5. Southeast Asian Islanders Walking in the Light	45
6. Southeast Asian Mainlanders Living in His Light	52
7. Lands Down Under See a Great Light	57
8. Pacific Islanders Shining in the Son	62
9. Persecuted Nazarenes Let their Light Shine	83
10. A Bright Future for the Asia-Pacific Region	88
Call to Action	91
Pronunciation Guide	92
Notes	95

From 1994 until April of 2005, when he began as lead pastor at Lewiston, Idaho, First Church of the Nazarene, Dr. Brent Cobb served as the Asia-Pacific regional director for the Church of the Nazarene. Prior to this role, he served as the senior pastor of Seattle First Church of the Nazarene from 1989 to 1994. He also served as pastor of Nazarene congregations at Long Beach, California; Sacramento, California; Dallas, Texas; Butler, Missouri; and Versailles, Kentucky.

With his wife, Marty, Brent served for 10 years in South Korea from 1970 through 1980. During their first term of service, he worked as the director of Korea Nazarene Theological College, now Korea Nazarene University. During their second term of service, he served as the mission director.

Dr. Cobb earned the doctor of ministry degree from Northwest Graduate School (now Bakke Graduate University of Ministry) in Seattle, Washington, in 1995. He and Marty have three children—Skyler, Sara, and Adam—as well as two grandchildren named Sierra and Kadin.

Foreword

Celebration. O how Nazarenes love to celebrate. And we are good at it! Special events often bring us together. Dedications. Anniversaries. Reunions. Homecomings. Holidays. Assemblies. Conventions. We love to gather as a family—to share and learn, to feast and fellowship, to remember and reminisce, to recognize and affirm, to rejoice and praise the Lord. Celebration seems to be part of the Nazarene DNA.

The year 2008 is a milestone in the history of the Church of the Nazarene. On October 5 Nazarenes around the globe will celebrate 100 years as a holiness denomination. And what a celebration it will be as 1.6 million Nazarenes do what we do best! We will worship the risen Lord, and He will be glorified by our praise for His blessing upon our beloved church.

As I have traveled around the world during the past two years, I have observed God-honoring times of celebration:

- In Ethiopia as the Central District dedicated a five-story building as a house of worship, training center, and field office that was finished debt-free.

- In the Democratic Republic of the Congo where a pastor walked four days to attend the district assembly.
- In Japan where the church celebrated 100 years and elected the first female district superintendent.
- In a creative access area where the churches are celebrating 1,000 new believers every week.

Dr. Brent Cobb has authored a book that trumpets celebration—heralding God's redeeming work through the Church of the Nazarene in the Asia-Pacific Region during the past 100 years. The dynamic history of this area spans 10 decades—from Japan, entered before the denomination was officially organized, down to two creative access areas entered in 2003. The stories of the church's advance stretches across thousands upon thousands of miles. Today the message of full salvation is being proclaimed in 29 world areas of this vast region.

As you read this book, join the 100,000 Asia-Pacific Nazarenes as they celebrate. Rejoice at what God has done, is doing, and will continue to do. Yes, it's time to celebrate.

Dr. Nina G. Gunter
General Superintendent

Introduction

Zho, a Chinese Christian, teaches house church pastors. At the beginning of a course in missions, Zho alerted the students they would have opportunity to give an offering for outreach to people on the far side of earth—people needing the Savior. He urged the 40 pastors to join him in asking God what He wanted them to give in their first-ever missions offering.

On Friday, at a special service, the group praised God in song and asked Him to grant them generous hearts. They passed an offering box, and each person gave with joy. Two students quickly counted the offering and reported the total. Everyone cheered, knowing that the average offering each struggling, bivocational house church pastor had given was equal to two weeks' income.

Seeing a tiny box inside the offering box, Zho opened it and found a note and ring inside. He read the note aloud: "I gave little in the cash offering because I had little to give. This ring is my effort to give what is most precious to my wife and me. It was my first gift to my fiancé to express my love for her. Thanks for asking us to give sacrificially in response to Christ's Great Commission."

Stories like this are lived out daily in countries across the Asia-Pacific Region, home to a large percentage of the earth's underevangelized and completely unevangelized people groups. Much of the region is within the 10/40 window, a relatively small section of the earth's surface located between 10 degrees and 40 degrees north latitude.

The Asia-Pacific Region extends from Japan's northernmost island to New Zealand's southernmost island near Antarctica. It reaches from Myanmar's shared border with Bangladesh eastward across the South Pacific to Tahiti. In this region the church serves in 29 world areas with 45 districts and 14 institutions of higher education. Here are some interesting highlights about the Asia-Pacific Region:

- China, with more than 1.3 billion people, is the world's most populous nation.
- Indonesia, the world's fourth most populous nation, is predominantly Muslim.
- Thailand is the earth's most populous Buddhist nation.
- Papua New Guinea is the nation with the most languages and dialects—over 800.
- The Philippines, largely Roman Catholic, is open to the message of personal salvation.
- Korea sends out more missionaries per capita than any nation on earth.

Japan, known as The Land of the Rising Sun, was the first field of missionary endeavor for the denomination on the Asia-Pacific Region. "For from the rising of the sun even unto the going down of the same," God declares, "my name shall be great among the Gentiles" (Mal. 1:11*a*, KJV). The international date line runs through the region's east side where sunrise marks the dawning of each new day.

"But for you who fear my name, the Sun of Righteousness will rise with healing in his wings. And you will go free, leaping with joy like calves let out to pasture" (Mal. 4:2, NLT). The Sun of Righteousness is the *Son*—Jesus Christ. His coming to the nations brings healing and unquenchable joy.

I was privileged to serve, along with my wife, Marty, and our children, as a Nazarene missionary in Korea from 1970 through 1980; to direct Nazarene work among Southeast Asian refugees in California in the late 1980s; and to serve in Manila, Philippines, as Asia-Pacific regional director from 1994 through 2005. The Asia-Pacific Region is my second home.

I invite you to join me on this fast-paced journey to catch glimpses of the first 100 years of the Church of the Nazarene in the Asia-Pacific Region. Along the way, celebrate with me what God has done.

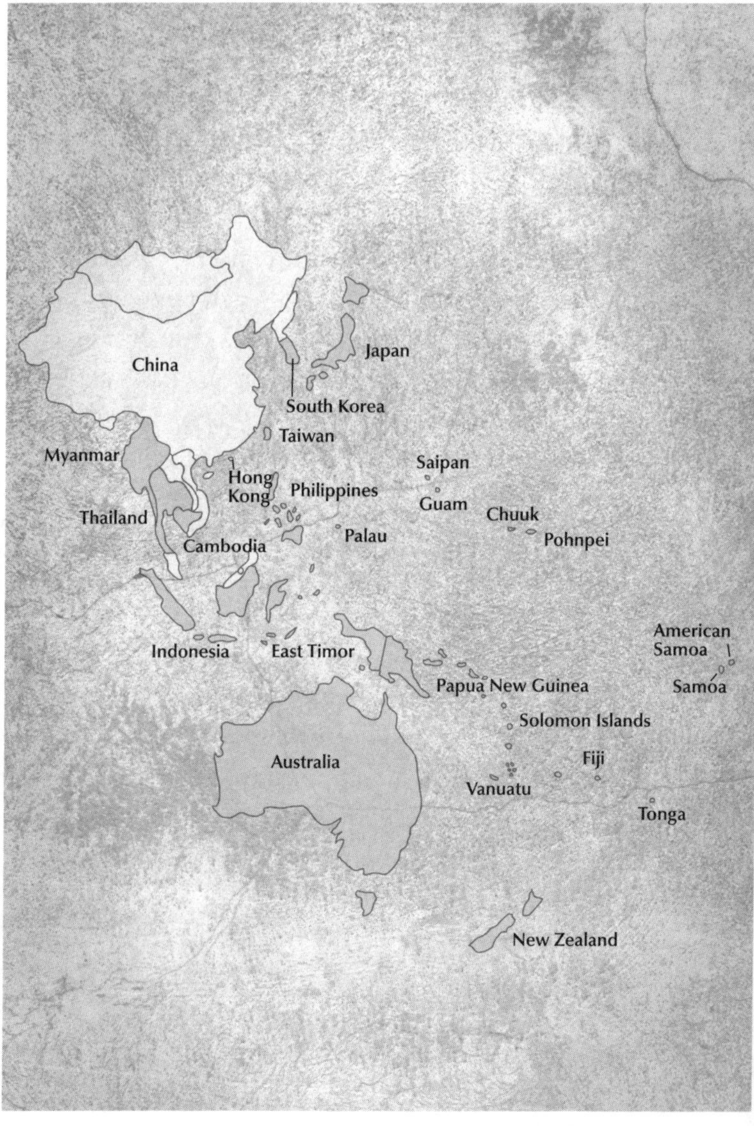
China
Japan
South Korea
Taiwan
Myanmar
Hong Kong
Philippines
Saipan
Guam
Chuuk
Pohnpei
Thailand
Palau
Cambodia
American Samoa
Indonesia
East Timor
Papua New Guinea
Samoa
Solomon Islands
Australia
Fiji
Vanuatu
Tonga
New Zealand

1
The Sun of Righteousness Shining in Japan

Mitsuko first encountered Christians as a high school student while attending an English Bible study in a missionary's home. Gathering with nine other Japanese young people every Saturday to read passages from the Bible sent her on a quest for true Christian faith. She devoured the songs they sang, like "When the Roll Is Called Up Yonder." And she sat enthralled as Mrs. Moore, the missionary, made the Bible stories come alive.

The students learned something new every week. Mitsuko especially admired the affection the 70-something Moores displayed for each other. Moore *Sensei* (respected teacher) whistled as he worked. He'd wink at his wife and give her big smiles. Mitsuko had never seen her dad wink at her mom or give her loving smiles.

Mrs. Moore urged Mitsuko to attend Shikoku Christian University where Moore *Sensei* had been founding president. Mitsuko took Mrs. Moore's advice. The university's godly professors influenced her greatly. One Christlike professor, who also happened to be blind, had earned his doctorate at Boston University. Another professor coached students in resisting unjust government practices. These teachers and others exemplified vital Christianity, and the campus community pulsated with a living, biblical faith.

Mitsuko went to a church where two other professors served as co-pastors. In her junior year she received the opportunity to study in Canada. Her pastors urged her to be baptized before leaving. She agreed, and before her baptism she genuinely entrusted her life to Jesus. After some time in Canada, God opened the way for her to join her boyfriend, Hitoshi, at Northwest Nazarene College (NNC) in Nampa, Idaho. NNC's people, as well those in College Church and the Nampa Nazarene community in general, accepted the couple and showered them with kindness.

Upon Hitoshi's graduation from college, he and Mitsuko were married. Dr. and Mrs. Grady Cantrell served as Mitsuko's Christian parents. Hundreds of people celebrated with them. They had never imagined people who weren't relatives showing such love to foreigners. Through them, and later through professors and students at Nazarene Theological Semi-

Hitoshi and Mitsuko Fukue

nary in Kansas City, they saw Christian faith in action.

The love Mitsuko felt from the missionary couple in her high school days, from Nazarenes in Nampa, and from others in Kansas City laid a firm foundation for her 30 years of Christian service. Early on, Mitsuko often asked Christians, "How can I repay you for the love you've shown me?" They answered, "Just pass along that love to others."

* * *

The Church of the Nazarene officially began in Japan in 1907. Early missionaries Minnie Staples and William Eckel worked closely with two Japanese leaders who had studied at Pasadena College in California. Their names were Hiroshi Kitagawa and Nobumi Isayama. For over 40 years Eckel served alongside Isayama who had even come to the dock to greet the Eckel family when they arrived in 1916.

Under Isayama and Eckel's leadership the district reached out to Korea in 1932. The two leaders visited Korea taking along an ethnic Korean pastor from the Japan District. They left him to plant the first Nazarene church in that country. Later they sent another Korean to start a second church so that by 1938 there were two Nazarene churches in Korea —the second in Seoul, present-day capital of South Korea.

The Japan District achieved regular district status in 1936. When Isayama and Eckel returned to Korea in 1939, Eckel reported that they "found the door wide open." He predicted the church in Korea would outgrow the church in Japan.

World War II devastated the church in Japan, leaving the denomination in disarray. Many Nazarenes had been killed or scattered and several buildings damaged or destroyed. Missionaries had been forced to leave. Eckel, who served as superintendent of the Rocky Mountain District in the United States during his wartime absence from Japan, returned in 1947. He urged the General Board to seize the moment and invest in the evangelization of Japan as General Douglas McArthur had urged all denominations to do. The church once again began sending many missionaries to Japan.

At this time, Japanese Nazarenes focused their energies and resources on educating pastors and laypeople. General Superintendent Orval J. Nease visited Japan in 1949 to reorganize the work while William Eckel secured from American occupation forces 45 properties for churches. Believing education was an important means of evangelism, district leaders began reaching out to the Japanese in the postwar era.

Japan Nazarene Bible College (now Japan Nazarene Theological Seminary) reopened in 1951 with a four-year curriculum to train people for pastoral ministry. In 1959, Japan Christian Junior College (JCJC) began on a 17-acre site with English and religion departments. The government approved graduates of the English program to teach in Japanese middle schools while graduation from JCJC's religion program became a requirement for entrance to Japan Nazarene Bible College.

Rev. Aoki asking for forgiveness for Japan's actions during the 1930s and 1940s.

Rev. Aoki requested to speak to the more than 2,000 Nazarenes from across the region. What followed next brought tears to everyone's eyes.

While time and space do not permit the stories of all Japanese leaders and missionaries to be told, one historic moment in the life of the Japan Church of the Nazarene must be noted.

The setting was the 1995 Asia-Pacific Regional Conference in Manila, Philippines. On Sunday morning, Japan District Superintendent Rev. Aoki requested to speak to the more than 2,000 Nazarenes from across the region. What followed next brought tears to everyone's eyes. Humbly and reverently Rev. Aoki asked them to forgive the Japanese people for the cruel treatment their country inflicted on much of Asia and the Pacific during the 1930s and 1940s.

Everyone was weeping, their hearts moved by their Japanese brother's sincere apology. Dr. Donald Owens led everyone in a prayer for reconciliation. People gathered around District Superintendent Aoki and all of the other Japanese Nazarenes, lovingly placing their hands on them as most people prayed out loud. It was evident to all the apology was accepted and love had won a victory over previous prejudices.

Today, Nazarenes in Japan have given well over U.S. $1 million for opening and supporting the work of the Church of the Nazarene in Thailand. They have sent their own missionary, Tomoyuki Hirahara, to Thailand to serve alongside his wife, Ceny (from the Philippines). And Japanese leaders have committed at least U.S. $200,000 to help with construction costs for the denomination's new Global Ministries Center in the United States. Many Japanese Nazarenes are catching a fresh vision and making a strong commitment to proclaim the church's message of holiness of heart and life throughout The Land of the Rising Sun.

2
Rays of Hope for Chinese People

China

Feng Lan-xin was the first Chinese doctor at Bresee Memorial Hospital in China. In 1936, while he was praying, Dr. Feng sensed God telling him to give thanks for the church at East Gate. Though East

Bresee Memorial Hospital in China

Gate was only three kilometers from his birthplace, he had never been there. Nonetheless, he began thanking God for the church at East Gate.

At vacation time Feng went home. He asked his father how many believers were in East Gate. "None," he said. *If there are no believers*, Feng wondered, *how is there a church? Why does God want me to give thanks for the church at East Gate?* He decided to go there to evangelize even though his dad said, "No one will believe. Our own village has only three believing families after 30 years."

Standing in the main street of East Gate, Dr. Feng began by singing about Jesus. Children gathered; then adults came. He told them about Jesus, then gave his own conversion story. A man invited him home. There, he and a friend put their trust in Jesus. During Dr. Feng's 1937 visit to East Gate many more people trusted Christ. Feng baptized 70 believers and formed them into a church. Through the years their children and grandchildren have given strong witness to Christ. Eventually, without hiring workers, the congregation built a new sanctuary, and over 1,000 believers attended its dedication. Today East Gate Church is a lighthouse and soul-saving center because Dr. Feng prayed, obeyed, and attempted the impossible in the power of the Holy Spirit.

The first Nazarene missionaries, the Peter Kiehns and Miss Glennie Sims, arrived in China in early 1914. They and other early missionaries labored faithfully with the conviction that Christ was building His Church, using them and their Chinese converts. They accepted responsibility for an area to which the gospel had not yet been taken.

These rugged pioneer missionaries introduced people to Jesus, made them true disciples, trained them for service, equipped them to plant churches, established a Bible college, and met needs through medical services and other compassionate ministries. They established a hospital, nurses' training school, and a home for unwed mothers and their children.

However, in 1941, when Japan's army invaded China, their presence posed a risk for their Chinese coworkers. As a result, the missionaries moved to a new area, leaving behind 54 organized churches, several preaching points, approximately 5,500 members, and 163 Bible college students. The Chinese pastors and students who remained enthusiastically expanded the kingdom of God and proclaimed the message of holiness.

By 1949, almost all missionaries had been forced out of China, leaving behind a growing church of perhaps 1.8 million members. Nazarene missionary Mary Scott, however, remained in China and soon ended up in a prisoner-of-war camp. While difficult, this experience gave her the opportunity to learn Chinese better and witness to everyone she could about the joy Jesus gives. Though she was imprisoned, her testimony about Christ's saving grace occasioned spiritual freedom for others.

When the Communist party under Mao Zedong closed its iron grip on China, brave Chinese Christians continued serving Christ behind the bamboo curtain. In an attempt to control China's Christians, the Communists established the Three Self Patriotic Movement that required churches to register or be closed. This birthed China's underground house church movement.

From 1966 through 1976, China suffered the tragedy of the Cultural Revolution, and waves of persecution engulfed China's Christians. But the martyrs' shed blood put heart into surviving Christians. The underground house church movement marched across China like a mighty army.

* * *

Bundled in layers of clothes, two women trudged through the snowy night. A light in the distance offered comfort as they leaned into the biting tempest.

Bitter blizzard winds blasted China's frozen farmlands. Bundled in layers of clothes, topped off by parkas with the hoods drawn close around their coal-black eyes, two women trudged through the snowy night. A light in the distance offered comfort as they leaned into the biting tempest. They hoped it was the light at their destination.

At midnight they saw the silhouette of a farmhouse and a man standing near the light. They approached, said a word, and he motioned them to enter the house. The man, however, stayed out in the storm. Between midnight and 2:30 A.M., 26 more people arrived at this center for pastoral training. Here, in the same place that our missionaries left in 1941, Nazarene pastors gather quarterly for "underground seminary."

The pastors waited patiently for their guest teacher, a Chinese-speaking Westerner who has been involved in pastoral training for over 20 years. They had invited him to teach about holiness, and promised to report to him what was happening at the grassroots level of China's church. They had also sent him security instructions and details about travel and timing.

The teacher's 14-hour trip ended with three pastors leading him down a silent, frozen road. They arrived at 2:30 A.M. The others greeted them warmly, praising God for bringing them all together safely.

After a brief sleep, they began hours of intensive training. A highlight for the guest teacher was hearing them report what God had done in the area since the missionaries left. They described God's presence through their seasons of imprisonment, His calling them to pastor secret congregations, the Holy Spirit's working through them in supernatural ways, and a great ingathering of people coming to Christ. They painted word pictures of church planting miracles that have glorified Christ and drawn people to Him.

The teacher then asked them how many churches were in the area. They reported more than 1,000. One of the students serves as mentor to 60 other pastors, and another mentors over 200 bivocational pastors.

Nazarene investment in China has yielded high dividends. Since 1941, 54 churches have produced more than 1,000 other churches, and 5,500 members have generated over 150,000 true followers of "the Nazarene" in the area where the Church of the Nazarene labored.

Taiwan

As Communism gained control of much of China's mainland, many people fled with the Nationalists under General Chiang Kai-shek to the island province of Formosa (Taiwan). Nazarene missionaries to Taiwan, the Millers and Holsteads,

Chinese women at worship

arrived in 1956, and the Renches in 1959. John Holstead established Taiwan Nazarene Theological College (TNTC) in a rented house in Taipei. In 1960 he found a large piece of land in the suburbs of Taipei, and TNTC and the district office have been there ever since. Several missionaries served as president of TNTC with the task of training pastors.

The Taiwan church struggled with self-support, long remaining dependent on the international church for help. In 1972, Paul Hwang, born on the mainland and converted in Taiwan, became the first

Chinese president of TNTC. Pan Ming-ding became the first national district superintendent of Taiwan in 1975.

A bright spot for the Taiwanese church is the opportunity for several Nazarene pastors to travel to the mainland to teach.

Many stirring stories exist that read as though they are right out of the Book of Acts, stories about Taiwan Nazarenes God is using in many places among the Chinese people. But for the sake of the safety of local Christians in those places, we cannot put those stories into written form. Pray for Taiwan's Nazarenes and the wide door of evangelism and service that is open to them today.

Hong Kong

After serving for years in Taiwan, learning Mandarin Chinese, John and Natalie Holstead sensed God's call to Hong Kong. In 1974, the Church of the Nazarene sent them to establish the church there. Early on, however, they realized a major challenge the church faced in that expensive, world-class city was locating and affording strategically placed properties for church planting.

In 1990, Nazarene Missions International chose Hong Kong for a global offering in observance of the Society's 75th Anniversary. The U.S. $750,000 goal was the highest ever for a denomination-wide offering. Urgency in giving came from the fact that this British crown colony would revert to China in 1997, and acquisition of church properties needed to happen fast.

A global prayer effort supported this initiative. By the time the offering was counted at the general treasurer's office in Kansas City, the total amounted to more than U.S. $885,000.[1] With these funds, John bought choice properties so congregations could minister to a greater number of Chinese people when Hong Kong became a "special administrative region" of China. When that time finally came, Hong Kong Nazarenes had devised creative strategies to continue growing even if government-imposed restrictions began to be placed on the church.

Nazarenes in Hong Kong are positioning the church to reach vast numbers of people. The potential abounds for Hong Kong Nazarenes to provide training for pastors in the mainland and to partner with mainland Christians in the Back to Jerusalem movement—a thrust to evangelize all people groups between China and Jerusalem.

3
A Light for the Nations Shining from Korea

By the late 1940s, the Church of the Nazarene in Korea was beginning to flourish. General Superintendent Orval Nease visited South Korea to grant elder's credentials to 7 pastors, receive 9 fully organized churches into the denomination, and welcome 835 new members. Robert Chung, a Korean graduate of Asbury College in Kentucky, soon arrived to develop the denomination in Korea. It wasn't long until the Korean War broke out, however, and Chung fled to the United States—barely escaping with his life.

For three years, the Chinese Communist army along with the North Korean Communist troops warred against the South, devastating the Korean peninsula and its people. When the war finally ended with a truce in 1953, Chung returned to find church buildings damaged and members scattered. Sadly, many Nazarenes had been killed. Chung felt it was now time for a missionary couple to come to Korea.

Donald and Adeline Owens were that chosen couple. In 1954 they set foot on Korean soil and soon established a Bible training school in a rehabilitated building in Seoul. Classes began with 23 students, 8 of whom were pastors. The first Korea district assembly was held in August 1955 with the election of Rev. Kee-suh Park as district superintendent. During his five-year tenure, membership rose to over 2,000 and the number of churches grew to 39.

During the next 11 years, the church in Korea grew exponentially gaining 6,155 members in 70 churches. The district then set a goal of starting 15 new churches during the next quadrennium. Within 2 years, 20 new churches had already been established.

Sadly, however, conflict between new and long-term leaders of the church curtailed that growth. At the 1970 district assembly, a bitter clash brought further division. Nazarenes in Korea and other parts of the world prayed for a spirit of forgiveness, reconciliation, and renewal to restore the rift and reignite evangelism. It was obvious they needed a fresh visitation by the Holy Spirit.

D r. Owens removed the outer wrapping from a package he said contained a portrait of the person responsible for the trouble. He then asked if anyone would like to see it.

In August of 1971, all of the Korean pastors and three missionaries gathered for a fellowship meeting. In one of the evening services, Donald Owens spoke from John 17:20-21 (RSV), "I do not pray for these only, but also for those who believe in me through their word, that they may all be one; even as thou, Father, art in me, and I in thee, that they also may be in us, so that the world may believe that thou hast sent me."

As he preached about Christ's passionate desire for His Church to be unified, he removed the outer wrapping from a package he said contained a portrait of the person responsible for the trouble. He then asked if anyone would like to see it.

Everyone eagerly answered yes. One by one Dr. Owens revealed to each person a framed mirror. Christ's Spirit brought conviction and godly sorrow. Tears of forgiveness soon accompanied warm embraces, and the group stayed for a night of prayer. It was the beginning of healed relationships and authentic revival.

At the March 1972 district assembly General Superintendent Orville Jenkins ordained 19 ministers in an atmosphere of loving unity. He appointed a task force to study the feasibility of creating two districts to foster growth and church planting. In 1973, under General Superintendent Eugene Stowe's leadership, the districts were set up as the Central District and the South District. Their hope is that one day the northern area will open to the church and become the North District.

Establishing two districts with their own excellent leaders set the stage for unprecedented growth that made up for the lost years between 1970 and 1973. Both districts planted churches in areas of Korea still without the salvation message. In 1974 the Church of the Nazarene in Korea gained 9,406 new members and planted 33 new churches.

Soon the Bible training school received accreditation. At the request of Korea's Ministry of Education, it relocated outside of Seoul due to the city's rapid population increase. The land on which the school had been built in the 1950s had been purchased with U.S. $5,000 Alabaster funds. It sold for approximately U.S. $5 million.

The church purchased a large tract of land further south in Cheonan City, an area targeted as a center for higher education. Today Korea Nazarene

Korea Nazarene University

University (KNU) has more professors with earned doctorates than the school had students in 1979. The total number of students in campus-based studies, extension classes, distance education, and adult education programs is more than 6,000. KNU is the premier university in Korea to provide quality education to physically disadvantaged students as well as provide programs to equip others to teach and minister to disadvantaged people.

In addition to the good reputation KNU has earned for the Church of the Nazarene in Korea, a Korean-language radio program called *Holy People of*

A Korean woman praying

God broadcasts three times weekly throughout the entire Korean peninsula and beyond. The program is also on the Web, allowing access at any time. KNU professors and the Korea district superintendent have committed themselves to supporting this ministry. One church even pays 50 percent of airtime costs.

Korean Christians have a heart to take the gospel to unreached areas. Today, South Korea sends out more missionaries per capita than any other nation. Behind them are the massive prayer support and giving network for which Korean Christians are noted.

4
Beautiful Beams Radiating from the Philippines

The youngest of 12 children, Julieta Macainan attended Roman Catholic schools while growing up in her native Philippines. Eventually she earned a bachelor's degree in commerce with a management emphasis.

During her sophomore year in college, a friend took Julie to church where she witnessed people praying and worshiping in a different way. This greatly impressed her. The Holy Spirit began creating in her a hunger to know Christ personally. After that experience, she felt convicted when she became easily upset or used bad language. She began longing for self control.

Following college, Julie worked for an economic development foundation. A Christian coworker invited her to an InterVarsity Christian Fellowship Bible study, and Julie's hunger for a personal relationship with Jesus Christ grew.

At work, Julie's boss made her the assistant general manager and sent her by ferry to Manila—the capital of the Philippines—to receive further training. On board the boat were three Americans: Flora Wilson and her daughters, Elizabeth and Brenda. These ladies struck up a conversation with Julie. Julie was surprised to hear them speaking her own language, and she also welcomed the opportunity to practice her English.

The kindness of the women increased Julie's craving to know Christ personally. She thinks of that day as the beginning of her conversion. One month later, she boarded the same ferry to Manila for another trip, and to her delight she heard Flora Wilson call her name.

This time, Flora used the long voyage to talk with Julie about a personal relationship with Jesus. Julie's hunger was written all over her face for Flora to read. Julie asked about the Church of the Nazarene and learned that a new church was being planted in her town. In fact, it was just one block from where she lived.

Upon returning home, Julie went to the Nazarene church—in a rented storefront—to introduce herself to pastor Jerry Tingson and the other joyous Nazarenes. She told them she'd met their missionary, Flora Wilson. They welcomed her to the church family with open hands and hearts and made her promise to come again on Sunday.

Julie didn't breathe a word of this to her family, however. If her mom had known she had gone to a Protestant church, she would admonish Julie by saying, "Always remember, your brother is a priest."

When Sunday came, Pastor Tingson preached a simple, clear salvation message to about 80 people. As soon as he gave an invitation for seekers to come to the altar, Julie went. Jesus became her personal Savior that morning, and her heart felt as though it would burst with joy.

For a while Julie tried to keep her new life in Christ a secret from her family. But when it was no longer possible, she told them the truth. Her mother threatened to disinherit her. It was terribly difficult to live in a home where the family opposed her commitment to Christ. Often at meals she had to leave the table, rushing to her room in tears.

Yet, rather than separating her from her Lord, the conflict caused her to cling more closely to Christ. In her Bible study, Julie was captivated by Christ's words, "The harvest is plentiful, but the workers are few. Ask the Lord of the harvest, therefore, to send out workers into his harvest field" (Luke 10:2). She began to sense God's call to prepare for full-time service.

Visayan Nazarene Bible College

When Julie talked with the Wilsons about her call, they urged her to come to Visayan Nazarene Bible College (VNBC) in Iloilo City. As soon as she could make arrangements to quit her job, Julie enrolled at VNBC. From her first day on campus her thirst for knowledge was insatiable. In her doctrine of holiness class, taught by Stanley Wilson, she responded to the invitation to kneel and completely consecrate her life to Christ. The Holy Spirit came in fullness, purifying her heart by faith.

About two months before she graduated, Dr. and Mrs. Kenneth Rice came to VNBC to conduct a Sunday School workshop. Out of the many pastors, professors, and students attending the workshop, they felt impressed to help Julie go to the United States for advanced studies.

In 1979, Julie began attending Nazarene Theological Seminary in Kansas City. She stayed in the home of the Rices and worked in the Sunday School Ministries Department at Nazarene Headquarters. Upon completing the master of religious education degree in 1982, she returned to teach at VNBC and became registrar. At this time, the missionaries teaching at VNBC were searching for an ideal place to relocate the Bible College so it could expand. Plus, water in Iloilo City was unsafe and VNBC was poorly located for serving the major island groups of the Philippines.

In 1986, VNBC relocated to Cebu, the second largest city in the Philippines, and its enrollment shot to a record high. Julie not only taught and served as registrar, but she began working on a doctorate in education. She became the first woman in the Philippine Church of the Nazarene to earn a doctorate degree.

In 1987, Dr. Julie Macainan became the first national president of VNBC. She has also served on the Asia-Pacific Nazarene Theological Seminary board of trustees, chaired the Philippine National Board for the Church of the Nazarene, served as secretary of the Board of the Asia Theological Association (representing over 70 institutions of higher education in 14 nations), and served as president of the Philippine Association of Bible and Theological Schools. She married Joel Detalo Jr., and today Dr. Julie Macainan Detalo gives dynamic leadership to VNBC.

Julie's story is only one of many Filipinos whose lives declare the praises of God and show the difference the Church of the Nazarene is making in their tropical homeland. Yet the task is not always easy. In Metro Manila alone, home to 16 million people, the church faces challenges, such as:

- How to reach over 5 million squatters
- How to serve some of the 10,000 people moving into Metro Manila weekly
- How to rescue some of the thousands of child prostitutes (over 60,000 in the Philippines)
- How to show Christ's love to homosexuals (Manila, the city, and the Philippines, the nation, have the world's highest ratios of acknowledged, practicing homosexuals.)

The Church of the Nazarene in the Philippines uses coaching networks across the 11 districts to equip and empower pastors to bring people to Christ, make them strong disciples, and lead them in church-planting ventures. *JESUS* film evangelism, use of the EvangeCube, evangelism through technology,

Brent and Marty Cobb with a Filipina and her three daughters

Work and Witness teams, mobile medical clinics, and many other means are also being used to bring Filipinos to Christ and equip them for effective service.

The Church of the Nazarene in the Philippines is growing rapidly, and Filipino missionaries are even serving in other world areas. The denomination's investment in this island nation has yielded good returns.

5
Southeast Asian Islanders Walking in the Light

Indonesia

"I just got a call from home. My father is dead!"

A professor at Indonesia Nazarene Theological College (INTC), Johannis stood weeping at his profound loss.

"Dead, how can that be? What happened?" asked the missionary.

"He was shot," Johannis explained. "He probably died immediately. Brother Larry, he knew he was going to die."

Two religious groups in the region Johannis called home had been at war several years. As a result, over 2,000 people had died and tens of thousands were missing and presumed dead.

Johannis's dad, a strong lay leader of a large church, was a winsome witness for Jesus. This, however, made him a marked man with a price on his head. In fact, one religious group paid people to cut off Christians' heads, literally, and bring them in.

While Johannis's father wouldn't fight, he cared for the wounded, buried the dead, and comforted the grieving. The day of his death, someone had called him to a trouble spot where he was shot three or four times. Those who shot him then tried to remove his head, but some Christians fearlessly stopped them.

To go there could mean Johannis's own funeral would follow. But as the oldest of six children, he knew it was his duty. His wife stayed behind with their children, waiting for news. He'd be in the danger area for three days . . . or so they thought.

The day Johannis arrived home the airport was attacked. Planes had to be flown out of harm's way and the airport secured before they could land. Later, when Johannis was ready to leave, the airport was attacked again. While he could leave the island by ship, he knew killers were onboard all ships looking for Christians.

Johannis, learning *he* was a target, returned to relatives' home, passing burned-out homes and churches. Days later he heard about a flight to Papua, the opposite direction of home but away from danger. Friends put him in the back of a truck with 20 others to keep the enemy from recognizing

Johannis, principal of INTC

him. Johannis boarded the plane just as it was about to take off.

Some days later Johannis arrived back at INTC. The entire campus community gathered to hear him tell about families losing fathers, brothers, sons.

But he was not bitter. "I saw what hate does to people," he said. "At Dad's funeral, attended by thousands, I saw what love does. I told everyone Dad wouldn't have wanted us to hate or avenge his death. He would have wanted us to forgive."

Today Johannis is the principal of INTC. Though there's often violence against Christians in his home area, he advocates nonviolence. He longs for those who hate Christians to come to know Christ. Indonesian Nazarenes like Johannis are a strong force in advancing the kingdom of God in their country.

East Timor

Situated on the eastern half of the large island of Timor, East Timor is located some 400 miles northwest of Australia. Formerly a province of Indonesia, the people's struggle for independence was long and difficult.

In 2001, the church entered this newly independent nation. A partnership between the Asia-Pacific regional office team, Nazarene Compassionate Ministries, and Nazarene leaders in Papua New Guinea and Indonesia launched the work. Warren and Janet Neal, medical missionaries, moved from Papua New Guinea (PNG) to East Timor to lead a community-based, health-care ministry.

Nazarenes in PNG also sent Michael and Jenny Mann, teachers at Melanesia Nazarene Bible College, as their missionaries. Acy Lodja, from an area of Indonesia where the language of East Timor is spoken, soon joined the Neals and Manns. Now married, she serves alongside her husband in this nation.

Acy Lodja, Indonesian missionary to East Timor

In April 2006, Nazarene Extension Bible School, affiliated with INTC, began in East Timor with 11 men and 6 women taking intensive courses.

Internal strife continues to plague East Timor, and civil war could break out at any moment. The global Nazarene family must pray for its brothers and sisters in East Timor, both for their safety and for Christ to use them to build His church.

Singapore

Perhaps no other area in the world is as clean, efficient, and nearly crime-free as Singapore. A modern city-state of 4.4 million people, it is a global shipping, banking, and mass communications center. Its educational system is excellent. Employment is high. Tens of thousands of South Asian workers have poured into Singapore, invigorating the economy.

In 2006, the Asia-Pacific regional office relocated from Manila to Singapore. Under the leadership of Verne Ward, a team of four couples arrived. This move has already improved travel options, expedited communications, and helped the church begin work in Singapore, Malaysia, and Brunei.

Regional Director Ward envisions developing dialogue groups or seeker Bible studies that will, in time, become believer Bible studies. He believes God will call some from these groups to lead the Church of the Nazarene in Singapore.

For years people who have moved to Singapore contacted Nazarene leaders to ask the church to come. Many of these individuals came in contact with the Church of the Nazarene elsewhere, including through radio broadcasts.

They were hungry for the church's message of holiness of heart and life. Now Nazarenes are equipping Singaporeans to herald the message of hope and winsomely model Spirit-filled lives to others.

Malaysia

Culturally, economically, and religiously Indonesia and Malaysia share much in common. Even their languages have similarities. As a result, Indonesian Nazarenes are currently devising strategies to plant the church in Malaysia. They are able to move about freely in this country, taking the church's message of full salvation with them.

> The nations of Southeast Asia's islands are strategic to the world of commerce, culture, and religion.

With Nazarenes now in Singapore—close to the heavily populated parts of Malaysia—and with many Malaysians coming to Singapore to work, contacts are also made in this way. God is paving the path for the Church of the Nazarene to grow in this Asian nation.

* * *

The nations of Southeast Asia's islands are strategic to the world of commerce, culture, and religion. To bring many Southeast Asian islanders to the Savior is a high priority of the Church of the Nazarene. A majority of them are without knowledge of Christ. The regional leadership team prayerfully focuses on areas of greatest need, devising strategies to enter those new areas, and making plans to establish churches in those places.

6
Southeast Asian Mainlanders Living in His Light

Myanmar (formerly Burma)

Seventeen-year-old Robin, a Buddhist, visited a friend's church. He heard the salvation story and trusted Jesus as his Savior. As a result, his father expelled him from the home. But after three months of praying for his family, Robin's parents also came to faith in Jesus.

God soon called Robin to full-time Christian service. Because missionaries had been expelled from Myanmar and Christian training centers had been closed, there was no place for him to prepare for the ministry. He decided to write to a Bible college in India and soon received an invitation to study there for free . . . if he could just get there. In those days no one was allowed to leave Myanmar.

At great risk, Robin crossed into East Pakistan (now Bangladesh) in order to get to India. At one

Robin Seia, founder of the Church of the Nazarene in Myanmar

point he walked for seven days. Then he caught a train to Calcutta and eventually arrived in Madras. There he lived with a missionary while learning the language. He heard about the Church of the Nazarene, read some of its literature, and found its teachings appealing.

Later, while studying at Fuller Theological Seminary in California, Robin attended and joined Pasadena First Church. In 1985 he returned to Myanmar to establish the work of the church in his homeland. It is now a viable denomination whose holiness message is bringing hope to thousands in Myanmar.

Thailand

Thailand, a strong Buddhist country, has the world's longest-reigning monarch as well as the distinction of having never been conquered by a foreign power.

The Church of the Nazarene entered Thailand in 1989 with the arrival of missionaries Michael and Rachel McCarty. We have two districts—one is primarily composed of ethnic Thai people, and the other is mostly made up of hill tribal people. On both districts lives are being transformed by God.

> The two men in white robes gazed into the witch doctor's eyes and announced, "The true and living God is going to send a messenger. Heed his message."

Jasuh, for example, was a young powerful witch doctor in a Lahu tribal village. As he sat on the porch of his bamboo house looking down the river one day, he saw two men in white robes striding toward him on the surface of the water. Coming to where he was, they gazed into his eyes and announced, "The true and living God is going to send a messenger. Heed his message because he will tell you how to know God." Then they left as quickly as they had come.

Soon a Lahu evangelist on his way to a village downstream stopped in Jasuh's village. According to Lahu custom he asked permission to stay the night, and Jasuh welcomed him into his home. After dinner, the evangelist took out a View-Master to help tell a Bible story.

The first picture Jasuh saw was from the story of Moses. To his surprise, the picture showed the two men he'd seen on the river. The witch doctor exclaimed, "I've been waiting for you to come. The two men in this picture told me to believe your message. What must I do to know God?"

The evangelist had never received such a reception from a witch doctor. He changed his plans and, instead of going downstream, stayed to teach Jasuh. Soon Jasuh and his entire family trusted Christ as their Savior. Missionary Samuel Yangmi came to his house to burn all his evil spirit shelves. Jasuh was soon baptized—the first in his tribe—and today Jasuh is an outstanding Nazarene pastor among his people.

Also in northern Thailand, *Hope in This Life* radio program leads AIDS sufferers to new life in Christ. As the program celebrated its first anniversary on the air, a number of people suffering from AIDS believed the gospel and became regular participants in the Nazarene church.

From Thailand, contacts have been made and work established in northern Myanmar and southwestern China. The work in both of these areas is fully legal, partly because of a partnership Nazarene Compassionate Ministries entered into with local leaders. NCM projects in these areas help open people's hearts to Christ and His message of hope.

Cambodia

Nazarene work in the land of the Killing Fields began in 1992 when Cambodian refugees who'd come to Christ in the United States returned to their homeland taking with them the message of holiness. Dangers and internal complexities in Cambodia make traditional ways of establishing the denomination difficult and innovation is necessary. As a result, many Cambodian Nazarenes in various parts of North America continue to make visits back home to help form Nazarene congregations out of family members and friends they lead Christ. They are striving to make them into true disciples as well as teach Nazarene beliefs and practices. Let's be sure our prayers go with them.

7
Lands Down Under See a Great Light

When Billy Graham traveled to New Zealand for an evangelistic crusade, Grandma Hannah took little David to one of the services. Along with thousands of others, he trusted Jesus as his personal Savior.

Years later, David said, "Nana became my mentor. She begged my mom to take her six sons to the Pacific Islanders Church in Auckland, made up of people from various South Pacific islands." But it turned out that the people there smoked, drank, and chewed addictive beetle nuts. So Nana took David and his brothers to Otara Church of the Nazarene where they met church planters, Frank and Joan Ranger. Their Spirit-anointed message made Nana's heart leap for joy. She shared it with everyone who would listen. She and David became charter members and plunged into the church's activities. With gusto the congregation proclaimed the good news of holiness of heart and life.

Missionaries Oliver [Ollie] and Evelyn Bartle mentored young adults struggling to walk with Christ. They often invited David and other young people to their home for meals and theological discussions. They urged them to consecrate themselves to Christ to be cleansed and filled with His Spirit.

Ollie prayed with David and painted attractive "faith pictures" of God's planned future for him. Of those days, David says, "I'd take two steps forward and one step back, but Ollie kept strengthening my faith, expressing confidence in me, and giving me godly counsel. Finally, I fully surrendered my life to Jesus. His blood cleansed me, and His Spirit filled me and equipped me for service."

For many years, David has served Christ along with his wife, Yvonne, and their four children. He is currently minister of music and youth in a Nazarene church in Sydney, Australia. He is also NYI president for the Asia-Pacific Region and the Asia-Pacific regional NCM coordinator. David leads joint Youth in Mission teams from Australia, New Zealand, and the United States helping team members discover the joy of serving a hurting world.

God has given David a dream of expanding missions by using culturally diverse regional NYI teams to reach new generations of youth with the good news of freedom and joy in Jesus. He believes this is the key to thousands of pre-Christians coming to know Christ.

Australia

In 1922, a Scottish Nazarene gave a copy of the *Herald of Holiness* magazine to a Methodist preacher in Australia. The minister soon began praying for the Church of the Nazarene to come down under. While the church didn't officially begin there until 1946, Australians had long been drawn to the message of holiness of heart and life.

In 1944, at a prayer meeting in Brisbane led by A. A. E. Berg, an American serviceman in Australia testified to entire sanctification. Berg had met other Nazarene servicemen who also testified to a second work of grace, and he himself had experienced the fullness of the Holy Spirit.

This serviceman put Berg in touch with one of the general superintendents who arranged for him to be received into membership of the Warren, Pennsylvania, church. The Pittsburgh District granted him a preacher's license, and he became the first Nazarene Australian. He told his friend A. C. Chesson about the Church of the Nazarene.

Others seeking holiness joined Berg and Chesson in forming the Australia Church of the Nazarene. The general superintendents asked E. E. Zachary, Kansas district superintendent, to help with the work. During several visits to Australia between 1946 and 1948, he organized churches, held revival campaigns, trained in Nazarene administration, and laid the groundwork for a Bible college.[2]

Berg became district superintendent in the mid-1940s and persuaded other pastors to join the denomination. At the district assembly in December 1948, five were ordained as elders. Berg continued as superintendent until his death in 1979.

> With more than 1,000 Nazarenes on the three Australian districts, the church is maturing and gaining momentum.

In 1952, Dr. Richard Taylor set up a Bible college in Sydney to train pastors and workers. Later the college relocated to Brisbane, and today serves people from Australia, New Zealand, and the South Pacific. Approximately 40 on-campus students and 30 students at extension centers attend the school. And with more than 1,000 Nazarenes on the three Australian districts, the church is maturing and gaining momentum for growth and global outreach in the days ahead.

New Zealand

Nazarene work in New Zealand began in the early 1950s when God led the Roland Griffiths family to explore the possibility of serving as missionaries. When one of the general superintendents visited and held a four-day preaching mission, God's blessing upon the meetings produced many changed lives.[3] The Griffiths' labors to make converts into Christ's true disciples produced the first Nazarene church in New Zealand.

From the early days of church planting in Auckland have come outstanding Christian servant-leaders. They include:
- Dr. Neville Bartle, missionary for many years in Papua New Guinea and Fiji
- Annette Taft Brown, missionary to Samoa and educator in America
- Nick and Beverly Faataape, currently serving a multicultural congregation in Australia
- Dr. Stephen Bennett, former professor at Asia-Pacific Nazarene Theological Seminary in Manila

Auckland plays a strategic role as Polynesia's educational, travel, and cultural hub. Prayer support by the global Nazarene family is needed for the Church of the Nazarene to gain impetus for growth in New Zealand and exert influence throughout the region.

8
Pacific Islanders Shining in the Son

MELANESIA

Melanesia (Greek for "black island") is a region of the South Pacific Ocean extending from the eastern Pacific to the Arafura Sea, north and northeast of Australia. The term was first used in 1832 to denote an ethnic and geographical grouping of islands distinct from Polynesia and Micronesia. World areas in which the Church of the Nazarene serves in Melanesia include Papua New Guinea, the Solomon Islands, Fiji, and Vanuatu.

Papua New Guinea

Nearly 50 years after the Church of the Nazarene's birth as a denomination, the church entered Papua New Guinea (PNG). This venture was funded by the NMI 40th anniversary project offering. Much prayer and preparation preceded the sending of missionaries Sidney and Wanda Knox. They went "to preach the whole Word of God to the beautiful people of this country," Verne Ward told the 2005 General NMI convention delegates. "The goal was to reach remote mountain tribes with the message of God's love and grace."

On January 9, 1956 (incidentally, the same day Verne Ward was born), the Knoxes traveled to a remote area in the Western Highlands Province. Some of the people were barely emerging from a stone-age-type culture. The Knoxes settled at Kudjip village, nestled in a mountain-rimmed valley, to become acquainted with the people, learn their heart language, and make the story of Jesus known to them. Jesus' grace and power worked through the Knoxes to set sinners free.

Before long, however, Sidney learned he had cancer. Eventually it claimed his life, and his loss was felt by Nazarenes everywhere. Missionaries who came after the Knoxes pursued their pattern of disciple making with much success. Many PNG Nazarenes have also followed their example, leaving behind villages and settling among people of different dialects, customs, diet, and ways of thinking to bring Jesus to them.

Early missionaries responded with Christ's compassion to people's crying needs, starting health-care ministries and schools in various parts of PNG to relieve suffering and educate people. Nazarene Health Ministries, a cluster of community development and health services, is a national model other groups seek to follow. Its mission goes beyond meeting the needs of the sick to holistic transformation of society. Community development and public healthcare programs extend Christ's transforming touch to thousands of people.

The 100-bed Nazarene Hospital, built with proceeds from the NMI 50th anniversary project offering, opened in 1967. Each month approximately 3,000 people receive outpatient care, 300 critically ill are admitted for major care, 100 babies are delivered, 60 surgeries are performed, and 100 people put their trust in Jesus as their Savior.

Surgeon Jim Radcliff and other missionaries could earn large salaries elsewhere but happily serve Christ alongside their PNG colleagues. Physician Bill McCoy and his wife, Marsha, served as missionaries in Swaziland, Africa, before coming to Papua New Guinea. Dr. McCoy recounts the following story.

One evening, after a long day at the hospital, Bill came home to find Marsha anxiously awaiting his arrival. She told him he needed to call Carol Howard, the obstetrics specialist at the hospital, right away.

On the phone, Carol's words were punctuated with tears as she related the events of the previous 12 hours. She had been summoned to the hospital at

1:00 A.M. to help a laboring expectant mother. The baby was in a position that made a normal delivery impossible. Carol had awakened surgical team members and asked them to rush to the operating room for a caesarean delivery.

> The mother could no longer feel any movement from the baby. Nurses couldn't hear a heartbeat. An ultrasound scan confirmed their fears.

Before they operated, however, Carol examined the mother and unexpectedly found the baby in a normal position. So she canceled the surgery, and the surgical team members returned to their homes to sleep. Around 7:00 in the morning, however, the baby had again moved out of position, and now there were far worse complications. The mother could no longer feel any movement from the baby. Nurses couldn't hear a heartbeat. An ultrasound scan confirmed their fears.

Carol was devastated and asked Dr. McCoy to perform the surgery. Carol stepped out of the room to tell the family about the baby's death. Before operating, Bill and his assistants prayed for comfort for the family and for Carol. Then he made an incision and delivered the baby.

But what was that? Was that a slight movement

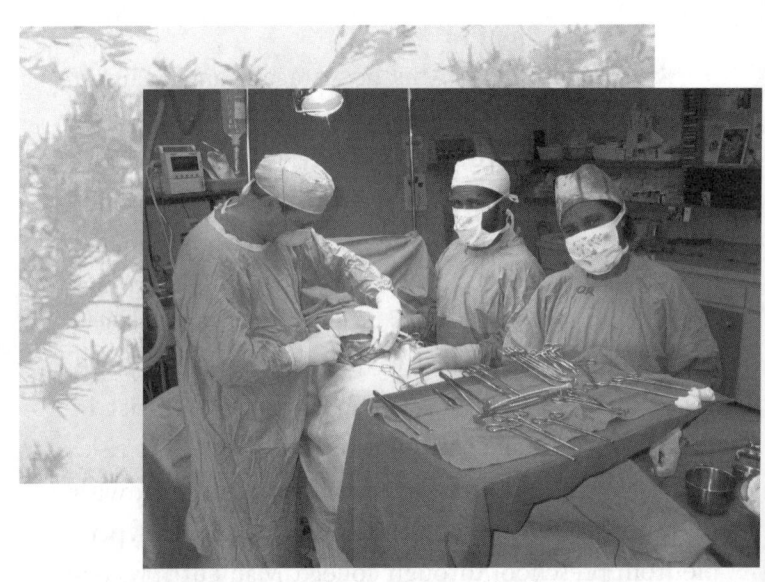

Doctors performing surgery at the hospital

he felt at the ankles? *No, just wishful thinking*, he told himself. A moment later, though, he wondered if his eyes were deceiving him when he laid the baby down and noticed a twitch of the baby's chin. Then there was another twitch. Bill glanced at Margaret, the scrub nurse, to see if she was seeing it. He saw the excitement in her eyes. "This baby is alive!" he exclaimed. "Mom, your baby is alive! Somebody go call Dr. Carol," he shouted.

Within minutes, the baby girl was crying a loud and strong cry. There were no complications. She was a miracle!

Scenes similar to this occur again and again at mission hospitals and birthing clinics in third-world countries where infant mortality is high. In many countries, families do not give babies a name until they've survived for a number of months. To name someone is to recognize him or her as a human being, to invest in the baby's life, to establish a personal relationship, and to become vulnerable. A name involves risk. Nazarene servants of Christ in Papua New Guinea are quite willing to take the risk.

Today, the Church of the Nazarene in PNG, with 12 districts, provides education for thousands of people from preschool through college. Many earn recognized degrees at Melanesia Nazarene Bible College (MNBC) and Nazarene College of Nursing. MNBC also offers a master's degree extension program.

In March 2006, General Superintendent Nina Gunter presided over the Western Highlands District Assembly with approximately 1,000 people from 130 churches and 14 preaching points. She ordained 3 women, a Nazarene first in PNG. Their ordination, along with 10 men, occasioned great celebration.

At the PNG Church of the Nazarene's 50th anniversary celebration in July 2006, the *Post-Courier* estimated the number in the opening march at 20,000. Everyone appraised the past with a profound sense of gratitude, but the focus was on what the church must become in the next 50 years. The chairman of the PNG national board challenged Nazarenes to pray and work in partnership to reach the goal of 100,000 members by 2016.

Solomon Islands

American missionaries Wallace and Mona White, along with Andrew and Lucy Moime—PNG's own missionaries—took the church to the Solomon Islands in 1992. This is an island chain several hundred miles east of PNG.

Today George and Nancy Miller serve in this area. They work with the pastors and members of 10 fully organized churches and preaching points.

When Dr. Gunter chaired the Solomon Islands District Assembly in March 2006, pastors and lay delegates reported significant progress despite the dangers in which they'd been living. An optimism of grace enables them to thrive through years of great civil strife.

Fiji

James and Joy Johnson, veteran missionaries to Samoa, moved to Fiji in 1995 to establish the church in this island nation. They followed up leads from Nazarenes in Samoa.

Later, Harmon and Cindy Schmelzenbach

Danielle Schmelzenbach with a Fijian child

arrived. Their teenage daughter, Danielle, tells of the ministry she's had in Fiji along with her parents:

> In the Fijian language I stumbled my way through the story of Noah's flood. I had a growing vocabulary but less-than-perfect grammar. My accent was decidedly American, giving the Fijian children many good laughs. When I'd arrived three years earlier, they teased me for being white, unable to climb the hill without help, unable to open a coconut, not knowing any songs they knew, and falling when crossing

the river on mossy rocks. Little children feared me; older ones unmercifully mocked me. I was different. Nothing I could do seemed to span the gulf of culture, language, and skills that separated us.

But God could do it. I asked Him to bring these children to accept this *kaivalagi* (foreigner).

Three years later I was helping the children act out a story in Fijian. Afterward, while doing crafts, little kids all asked me to help them. I could scarcely move with so many kids trying to sit in my lap, hold my hand, or braid my hair. I loved every minute of it.

God is a master bridge builder. He helped me build a bridge across a gulf that had been a barrier between the kids and me.

Today, the Fiji District is led by Spirit-filled Fijian Nazarenes. They are planting churches and proclaiming the message of holiness. From Fiji the church will inevitably reach into other island nations of the South Pacific.

Vanuatu

Papua New Guinean Nazarenes played a vital role in planning for the church's entry to Vanuatu, the neighboring island nation to their southeast. In May 2003, David Potter, along with Verne and

Natalie Ward, traveled to Vanuatu to arrange for David's family to deploy to this nation.

In 2004, months after the Potters began serving in Vanuatu alongside a highly focused Youth in Mission (YIM) team, they sent a letter to their prayer partners describing the Lord's work. The following is an excerpt from their correspondence:

> Have you ever witnessed the birth of a baby? We had the excitement this summer of witnessing new life in many of the young people of our community and the birth of a church. We saw the Lord . . . answer our prayer for the development of a youth group. One of the young ladies, raised in a pastor's home . . . admitted she had not been walking with the Lord. Now she has become bold in her witness for Jesus and is faithfully helping teach the children's Sunday School class.
>
> The first-ever NYI camp in Vanuatu was a great success. It was a perfect setting with a dining hall, dorms, a soccer field, and a beach for a big bonfire. Thirty-five people attended the weekend camp. The theme was . . . "We must walk in the light." In the camp's final session [one of the YIM team members] shared with the young people Christ's call for each of us to take His light into the world. This was followed

by a candlelighting service, which beautifully illustrated the light of Christ being shared from person to person.

Please pray with us for young people who have dedicated their lives to the Lord to continue to grow strong in their relationship with Him and daily to live 1 John 1:5-7.

Rejoicing in Him,

David, Sylvia, Jeffrey, and Wesley Potter

By March 2006, the Potters had officially registered the church in this group of 83 islands. Papua New Guinea then sent Peter and Jenny Isaac and their three sons as missionaries to Vanuatu. Peter and Jenny had both served as teachers at Melanesia Nazarene Bible College in PNG, and Jenny had recently been ordained. Joining the Potters, the Isaacs help in church planting, disciple making, and pastoral training. The Church of the Nazarene, with its holiness message, has bright prospects for healthy growth in Vanuatu.

POLYNESIA

Polynesia (Greek for "many islands") is a large grouping of over 1,000 islands scattered across the central and southern Pacific Ocean. Geographically, Polynesia is over-simply described as a triangle with its corners at Hawaii, New Zealand, and Easter Island.

Samoa

The Church of the Nazarene entered American Samoa in 1960 with the arrival of Jarrell and Bernice Garsee and their two small children. Immediately they plunged into language study to better serve the people.

Over the years, 12 other missionary families arrived to serve in various capacities for the church. While some stayed a short time, the Larry Duckworth family served in American Samoa for 20 years. James Johnson and his family have served here and elsewhere in the Pacific for over 25 years. James is now the field strategy coordinator for the Church of the Nazarene throughout Polynesia and Melanesia.

Samoa (formerly called Western Samoa) is located 90 miles west of American Samoa. Jarrell Garsee registered the church here in 1964, however new missionaries weren't allowed to come until 1971. Jerry Appleby and his family moved to Samoa at this time. Since most land is communal and owned by tribal chiefs, it truly was a miracle that Jerry was able to buy properties for the church including two acres of land for a Bible college.

Soon Samoa Nazarene Bible College was started. It has developed into the South Pacific Nazarene Theological College (SPNTC) based in Fiji. Several graduates of SPNTC have earned master's degrees at the seminary in Manila. One of them now serves as the principal of SPNTC. The free movement of Nazarenes around Polynesia has helped expand possibilities for the church to reach into new world areas.

Tonga

Tonga lies about a third of the way between New Zealand and Hawaii. Work here began in a backdoor sort of way when a retirement-age lay couple, Doc and Charmayne Old, arrived in 1994.

God directed Charmayne, a nurse, to seek the "hidden treasures" of Tonga—that is, the handicapped people of this island kingdom. Tongans view handicapped people as God's punishment for their parents' sins. Without records of their existence, without rights, and with few to care about them, they're lost to society. Their parents feel shame. Neighbors don't know they exist.

> God birthed in Doc and Charmayne a dream for a center for the handicapped. Today the Mango Tree Respite Center is a vibrant reality.

James Johnson visited Tonga to investigate how the church might begin here. A Tongan told James he knew Nazarene missionaries who already lived there. James told him no Nazarene missionaries lived

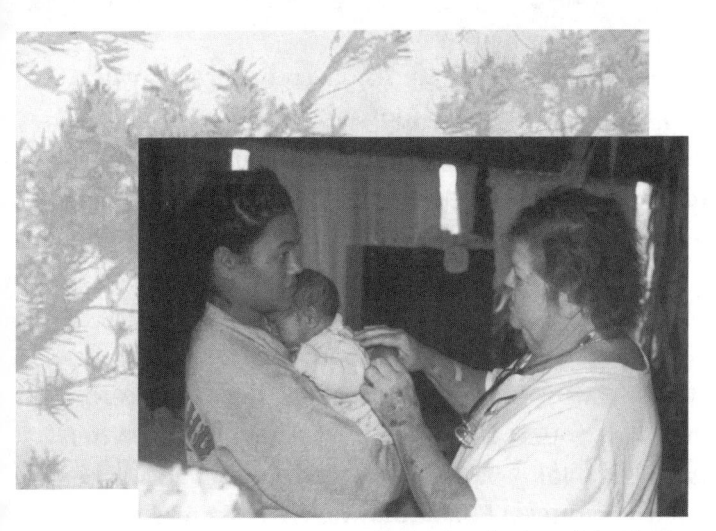

Charmayne checks an infant in Tonga

in Tonga, but the man insisted there were. He then proceeded to hand James their business card that read: "Doc and Charmayne Old, volunteer Nazarene missionaries."

God birthed in Doc and Charmayne a dream for a center for the handicapped. Today the Mango Tree Respite Center is a vibrant reality.

Harmon Schmelzenbach III participated in the dedication of the Mango Tree Respite Center—the fulfillment of the Olds' God-given vision. Large tents graced the front of the beautiful two-story building. Representatives from Tonga's royal family came, and radio and television crews broadcast the event throughout the nation.

Harmon and missionary colleagues from Canada and Korea crossed the main island visiting homes of the "hidden people" the Olds had found. One mom in her tiny shed home was caring for the needs of her son, his muscles atrophied, his head permanently drawn back, his mouth open. Yet his eyes sparkled. She told how alone she'd felt before the Olds found them, bringing them hope. When asked how long she'd fed, bathed, and cared for her son, the mom said the "boy" was 21 years old.

Another home included two brothers who were unable to care for themselves. One was in his 40s; the other in his 30s. One lay on the floor; the other was propped up in a wheelchair. Living conditions weren't good. The Korean missionary got down on the dirt floor with tears flowing, seeking to bring comfort to them. Long after the missionaries had left, he was still wiping away tears.

The Olds tirelessly campaigned for this marginalized segment of society, raised support, and registered the Church of the Nazarene. Today the incidence of cerebral palsy is down and the percentage of healthy Tongan children is up. For all of the handicapped in this nation, a day of dignity, love, and acceptance has dawned, traceable to God bringing the Olds to care for them.

While Charmayne has since gone to be with the Lord, the vision God gave this dedicated couple is still alive. What the Olds and others have done in Tonga is not unlike what God did for us in Christ—leaving heaven's beauty and purity, coming down to the unattractiveness of what we are at our worst, reaching out to us in love, giving us hope.

MICRONESIA

Micronesia (Greek for "small island") is the name of a region consisting of over 2,000 small islands spread over the western Pacific. Melanesia lies to the south, and Polynesia lies to the east.

Guam

An outreach of the Hawaii District brought the Church of the Nazarene to Guam in 1971. It was later assigned to the Asia-Pacific Region. For several years Guam First Church was the only Nazarene congregation in Micronesia.

In 1994, when I was serving as the regional director, I appointed Denny Owens as area coordinator for Micronesia. As a former missionary to the Philippines, I was confident he could help the church reach beyond Guam—the cultural, travel, and communications hub of Micronesia—to other islands.

Today the Guam Church of the Nazarene is strong. First Church is a multicultural congregation, and from its strategic location seeks to capitalize on its many contacts with other people from various island groups in Micronesia.

Palau

Denny Owens contacted Limitz Iyar from the newly independent Republic of Palau who was finishing up his studies at Nazarene Bible College in Colorado Springs. He was ready to plant the Church of the Nazarene on his native soil. Iyar and his family moved from Colorado to Palau in 1995.

The president of Palau soon appointed Iyar the national director of prison chaplaincy. While his long hours of work for the government have slowed the beginning of the first Nazarene church, Palauan Nazarenes in Guam First Church as well as in the United States have sensed God's call to assist with beginning Nazarene churches in this island nation.

Chuuk

The world area of Chuuk was targeted in 2000 for the church to enter. Rex Ray and Perlita de la Peret, Filipino Nazarene missionaries serving in Guam, arrived in the capital city of Weno to begin the Nazarene work.

Perlita grew up in a mountain tribal home in the northern part of the Philippines. Jesus became her personal Savior at a children's camp. Late in her

The de la Peret family serving as missionaries in Chuuk

life her father answered the call to pastoral service, and Perlita saw the sacrifice and energy with which her parents approached pastoral ministry.

Christ's Spirit living in Perlita has helped her overcome difficulties and empowered her to follow God's call for her life. Serving Christ brings her boundless joy as she experiences the Spirit's daily renewal to make her adequate in her work as a

Nazarene missionary. Many Filipino contract workers live in Chuuk with its more than 70 islands, and a number of them work in Weno First Church of the Nazarene. Along with her husband and two sons, Perlita is living a life of high adventure in the service of the King of Kings.

Saipan

Saipan is 1 of 14 islands composing an American commonwealth known as the Northern Mariana Islands. In 1995, Micronesia district superintendent Wayne LaForce made new contacts for the church in Saipan and began conducting worship services there. However, it wasn't actually declared a new world area for the church until 2000. As the core group of Nazarenes grew, Wayne contacted a Nazarene couple in Oklahoma to enlist their help.

Dave and Helen Ann Bucher came to Saipan as tentmaker missionaries and began teaching in public schools to support themselves. In September 2005 the Living Hope Church of the Nazarene they planted with the help of volunteers was officially organized.

Mission Corps teams and teachers have come to help the Buchers with Vacation Bible Schools and various other ministries. The church's message of holiness of heart and life has taken root in Saipan and is bearing fruit that will last.

Rev. Dave and Helen Ann Bucher with their daughter, Laura

Pohnpei

The church began work in Pohnpei in 2000 when Wayne and Connie LaForce were sent to work with Frank Santos, a Pohnpeian who had been converted in Guam. Frank and his family had stayed at Guam First Church after a typhoon destroyed their home. When they returned to Pohnpei, Wayne spent 15 months training Frank to be a pastor. The congregation of approximately 70 that Frank leads is a catalyst to plant other rural congregations throughout Pohnpei. A Work and Witness team from Bethany,

Oklahoma, helped these Pohnpeian Nazarenes build their own worship center.

A multicultural, English-speaking congregation also meets in the capital city. It was officially organized on Palm Sunday of 2006. Two Filipino families transferred from the Nazarene church in Chuuk and have given strong leadership to this congregation.

9
Persecuted Nazarenes Let their Light Shine

"We'll burn this house to the ground if the pastor doesn't come out," the mob screamed. Waving torches, they were eager for the believers' blood. Determined to stop Christ's Church, these shrieking fanatics had surrounded the house church during worship, brandishing sickles, machetes, and torches.

Though the group inside was terrified, some offered to go out instead of the pastor. But Pastor Hadu determined to plead for his people's safety. Cursing him, the angry mob demanded the Christians never gather again.

"I've got documents granting us permission to hold services," Hadu explained. "They're from the head of the Department of Religion."

"We don't care if they're from the president," the group shot back. "If you hold another service, we'll burn your house down."

Back inside, the churchgoers prayed passionately and planned to meet secretly in other believers' homes, trusting Christ's words, "Upon this rock I will build my church, and all the powers of hell will not conquer it" (Matt. 16:18*b*, NLT).

But when Pastor Hadu came out of his house the next morning, hostile neighbors were waiting to follow him. *What shall I do?* he wondered. *If I go to members' homes, I'll endanger them.* His wife left for the market and neighbors followed her. Hadu couldn't neglect his flock, so he went to one of their homes. An angry rock-clutching mob filled the yard, but God miraculously scattered them.

Many more deliverances from death proved God's presence. For instance, one day Hadu and his wife were hit by a truck while riding their motorbike. Critically injured, his wife laid unconscious in the hospital for days. The police told Hadu they knew who deliberately struck them, but nothing is done.

Some Christians in creative access nations have prices on their heads—literally. These are publicized prices to be paid for bringing in the heads of Christian leaders. The greater their Christian influence, the higher the price. Some of these individuals pay the ultimate price of martyrdom for their faithfulness to Christ.

God's Word is precious to persecuted Christians. They read, "Can anything ever separate us from Christ's love? Does it mean he no longer loves us if we have trouble or calamity, or are persecuted, or hungry, or destitute, or in danger, or threatened with death?" (Rom. 8:35, NLT).

To these questions persecuted Christians answer with the apostle Paul, "No, despite all these things, overwhelming victory is ours through Christ, who loved us. Nothing in all creation will ever be able to separate us from the love of God that is revealed in Christ Jesus our Lord" (Rom. 8:37, 39*b*, NLT).

Such words leap from the pages of Scripture for these joyous, suffering servants of their Master. His Spirit oversees Christ's suffering Church. Often where Christians pay the highest price the Church grows the fastest. Persecution is powerless to stop Christ's Church.

※ ※ ※

The following letter came from a veteran missionary couple serving in a creative access nation on the Asia-Pacific Region. They must be careful that their witness for Christ doesn't put local people at risk. Here's the letter in revised form with all names changed:

Dear Brent and Marty,

Yesterday was a day we'll long remember. Many of our family in the Lord gathered along the banks of a river. Pastor John had a battery-operated box that plays more than 200 hymns in the language of this nation. We sang "Glorious Freedom" and other songs.

Pastor John brought a powerful message about Christian baptism. The local Christians sat on newspapers on concrete steps. Each of the six baptismal candidates stood and gave their testimonies.

Stephen, a university student, had a Christian background. Mark was a close friend of Angela's for whom we've often prayed. Julia was one of my past graduate students. When she told me about her interest in knowing God, I invited her to attend our gatherings. She came, and the Holy Spirit began working in her heart. Rebecca surprised us when she spoke in front of the group since she'd always seemed shy. How beautiful it was to hear her describe the day she and Luke, her husband, came to our apartment and prayed to invite Jesus into their hearts. Luke, with a radiant face, told about his newfound faith and how Christ was helping him in his work as a welder. Aaron told about finishing reading with me *The Purpose Driven Life* and *Celebration of Discipline.* He'd had no interest in Christ in his early life, but the Holy Spirit drew him to faith in Jesus.

Dorothy read about baptism from the *Manual*. The six candidates repeated together the Apostles' Creed. We prayed, and then we all went down to the water. Swimmers moved aside to give us the best spot for the baptisms. The candidates came one by one to be baptized.

What a glorious celebration of Christ's transforming grace and power! Many pre-Christians closely observed it all. After the service, some came up to Iris and me to have their picture taken with us since young people in this nation like to have their picture taken with foreigners.

Our people gave people gospel pamphlets with Pastor John's name and phone number on them. We know that when you share this story you'll protect our local Christians here where there is opposition to house churches and the sharing of the gospel among "urban intellectuals," as they call university students and professors.

Yours in the Son,

Stan and Iris

10
A Bright Future for the Asia-Pacific Region

The first nation for the Church of the Nazarene on the Asia-Pacific Region was Japan. Today, Japanese Nazarenes are serving as global missionaries, going as volunteers for short-term service, and giving generously to support the global mission of the church. Pray for renewal in the local congregations that will give impetus to renewed evangelism and church planting in Japan.

The creative access nations on the Asia-Pacific Region show strong signs that they will be at the forefront of evangelism and mission in the next 100 years. Areas where persecution is severe are the very places where the church is growing best.

> In the first 100 years of the church's work on the Asia-Pacific Region, the number of members we're free to report is approximately 100,000.

Of the nations that can be put in print, Korea has the potential for sending the most missionaries. The Philippines is poised for great increase for the Church of the Nazarene while Nazarenes in Papua New Guinea are striving for 100,000 members by 2016. Details about areas of the Asia-Pacific Region with large Islam populations cannot be disclosed, however your prayers are needed. Pray that the Church of the Nazarene on the region will target and reach many Muslims for our Master.

In the first 100 years of the church's work on the Asia-Pacific Region, the number of members we're free to report is approximately 100,000. By 2025 the number will likely more than double. God is giving Asia-Pacific Nazarenes a vision of a great harvest of people for the Master.

General Superintendent Dr. Nina Gunter writes, "One need only hop island to island, nation to nation, and worship and fellowship with Nazarene believers to realize the impact of the local church in mission evangelism and support. As I traveled the Asia-Pacific Region for district assemblies and other gatherings, I discovered a strong corps of national leaders, missionaries, local church leaders, educators, and medical personnel, all bearing testimony to the faithfulness of God to bless our obedience to the Great Commission. Success is obeying God. The foundation and ministries of our first century are rock solid. I anticipate the second century to be even more blessed."

The stories you've read about Asia-Pacific Nazarenes who've answered God's call to salvation and holy living are but a small sampling of those available. Many more could be told of people associated with our churches in the region who've felt Christ's redeeming touch because local congregations of Nazarenes have been true to their God-assigned mission to make disciples among all nations.

From the rising of the sun on the eastern side of the region to the going down of the sun in the west, Asia-Pacific Nazarenes are lifting up Jesus, making known "the Son of Righteousness" across a sprawling region. They're proclaiming and putting into practice holiness for people's hearts and lives, and Christ is building His Church.

Call to Action

After reading this book, please consider doing one or more of the following:

1. Intercede for unreached people on the Asia-Pacific Region, home to over 2 billion men, women, and children. Many have not yet heard the good news of Jesus.

2. Consider an assignment in Japan, Korea, or China as an English teacher. Doors are wide open. It is a tremendous opportunity to influence the lives of future national leaders. Contact dhane@apnaz.org for more information.

3. Support Asia-Pacific schools with your prayers, teaching skills (if you are a qualified teacher), and your giving. For more information, visit these web sites:
www.nazarene.org/education/iboe/asiapacific/display.aspx
www.apnts.org/pages/index.php
www.kornu.ac.kr/kornu/eng/index_eng.html

4. In compassionate response to human need in Southeast Asia, sponsor a child at Thailand's Maetang Children's Home or support the *New Life for Thai* (AIDS) ministry. For more information, visit www.ncm.org.

5. Stay up-to-date on happenings in Melanesia and the South Pacific with these web sites:
www.kudjipnazarenehospital.org
www.fijiboat.org

Pronunciation Guide

Introduction
Papua — PAH-pew-ah
Zho — zhoh

Chapter 1
Ceny — SEN-ee
Hiroshi Kitagawa — hi-ROH-shee ki-tah-GAH-wah
Hitoshi — hi-TOH-shee
Mitsuko — mit-SEW-koh
Nobumi Isayama — noh-BOO-mee i-sah-YAH-mah
Pyongyang — PYUHNG-yahng
Sensei — SEN-say
Shikoku — shi-KOH-kew
Tomoyuki Hirahara — toh-moh-YEW-kee hee-rah-HAH-rah

Chapter 2
Chiang Kai-shek — chayng kai-SHEK
Feng Lan-xin — FUHNG lahn-zhin
Formosa — fohr-MOH-sah
Hwang — HWAHNG
Kiehns — KEENS
Mao Zedong — mou zay-DAHNG
Pan Ming-ding — PAHN meeng-deeng
Taipei — tai-PAY

Chapter 3
Cheonan — CHOH-nahn
Kee-suh Park — kee-suh PARK
Seoul — SOHL

Chapter 4
Cebu	se-BOO
Iloilo	ee-loh-ee-loh
Julieta Macainan	juw-lee-E-tah mah-cah-EE-nahn
Visayan	vi-SAI-yin

Chapter 5
Acy Lodja	AH-chee LOH-jah
Johannis	yoh-HAH-nis
Timor	TEE-mohr

Chapter 6
Jasuh	jah-SOO-ah
Lahu	LAH-hew
Madras	mah-DRAHS
Yangmi	YUNGH-mee

Chapter 7
Brisbane	BRIZ-ben
Faataape	FAH-ah-tah-ah-pay
Otara	oh-TAH-rah

Chapter 8
Arafura	ah-rah-FEW-rah
Bucher	BOO-cher
Chuuk	CHEWK
Fiji	FEE-jee
Gabriel Kaulo	GAY-bree-ehl kah-EW-loh
Kaivalagi	kah-ee-vah-LAH-gee
Kiribati	kee-ree-BAH-tee
Kudjip	KOO-jip
Limitz Iyar	LIM-itz EE-ahr
Luzon	lew-ZON
Malapoa	MAHL-ah-poh-ah
Mariana	mah-ree-AH-nah
Moime	MOH-ee-may

Palau	puh-LAUW
Perlita de la Peret	per-LEE-tah day-lah per-RAY
Pohnpei	pawn-PAY
Port Vila	pohrt VEE-lah
Saipan	sie-PAN
Schmelzenbach	SHMEHL-zhuhn-bah
Tebakor	tee-BAH-kor
Timor	TEE-mohr
Vanuatu	vah-new-AH-tew
Weno	WE-noh

Chapter 9

Hadu	HAH-dew

Call to Action

Maetang	MAY-dayng

Notes

1. John Holstead, *On This Rock* (Kansas City: Nazarene Publishing House, 1996), 65-66.

2. Franklin Cook, *Water from Deep Wells* (Kansas City: Nazarene Publishing House, 1977), 149-50.

3. Connie Griffith Patrick, *The Land of the Long White Cloud* (Kansas City: Nazarene Publishing House, 2003), 25.